扫描关注出版社微信公众号，
进入数字阅读发现更多资源

打开微信，扫一扫，
欣赏本书中英文朗诵

中华善字经

（汉英对照）

Three-Word Primer of Goodness

(Chinese-English Bilingual Edition)

尹飞鹏　著

赵彦春　译

Authored by Yin Feipeng

Translated by Zhao Yanchun

上海大学出版社

Shanghai University Press

图书在版编目（CIP）数据

中华善字经：汉英对照 / 尹飞鹏著；赵彦春译. —上海：上海大学出版社，2020.5
　ISBN 978-7-5671-3825-4

Ⅰ.①中… Ⅱ.①尹… ②赵… Ⅲ.①善—品德教育—研究—中国—汉、英 Ⅳ.①D648

中国版本图书馆CIP数据核字（2020）第049594号

中华善字经（汉英对照）
尹飞鹏　著　赵彦春　译

出版发行	上海大学出版社
社　　址	上海市上大路99号
邮政编码	200444
网　　址	www.shupress.cn
发行热线	021-66135112
出 版 人	戴骏豪
印　　刷	江阴金马印刷有限公司
经　　销	各地新华书店
开　　本	889mm×1194mm 1/24
印　　张	5 $^2/_3$
字　　数	113千字
版　　次	2020年5月第1版
印　　次	2020年5月第1次
书　　号	ISBN 978-7-5671-3825-4/D·224
定　　价	28.60元

策　　划	许家骏
责任编辑	王悦生
助理编辑	陆仕超
装帧设计	柯国富
技术编辑	金　鑫　钱宇坤

目 录

传世之佳作　扬善之心经（代序1）…………………… 1

逐善——读尹飞鹏《中华善字经》有感（代序2）…… 8

上篇………………………………………………………… 1

下篇………………………………………………………… 53

后记………………………………………………………… 105

A Verse Standing the Trial of Time;
   a Sutra Extolling Goodness (Introduction I) ·············· 4

Pursuing Goodness —— Reflections on *Three-Word Primer of Goodness* by Yin Feipeng (Introduction II) ·············· 13

Part I ·············· 1

Part II ·············· 53

Postscript ·············· 107

传世之佳作　扬善之心经
（代序1）

"善"作为中华文明最基本的组成元素，在传统文化中具有最重要的特质和核心价值，宣传和弘扬"善文化"是突出时代精神、构建社会主义核心价值观的客观需要。同时，善也是人性和人生态度的反映，内附于人的道德素养之中，外化于人的言行举止之上。

纵观古今，历代盛世无不是善治之为，育善扬善更是中华民族治家立业之本，传世的家训异彩纷呈，堪称经典。《颜氏家训》尽述行善立身治家之法，开家训之先河；《朱子家训》精辟地阐明了修身治家之道，也是一部家教名著，如"善欲人见，不是真善"等名句流传至今，脍炙人口。"人之初，性本善"，古之箴言诠释了善的含义，老幼皆知，给人以智慧的启迪；"积善之家，必有余庆"，影响了多少代人以积德行善作为治家理念；"勿以善小而不为，勿以恶小而为之"，启示着做人的道理。千百年来，善有传承，经久不衰，善的理念影响了一代又一代人。倡善之念，修善之为，是中华民族传统教育的核心。

中 华 善 字 经
(汉英对照)

善文化是人类文化的智慧结晶。善的历史可追溯到远古时期,与人类发展同行。然而其跨度之长,范围之广,不好提炼,难以表达。善的哲理光芒、经典论述大都是古人的研究成果,现在人们对善的实践多,对其内涵的研究少,系统的理论研究成果更少,时代需要善,时代呼唤善文化的经典大作。

金秋时节,有幸品读到了著名书法家尹飞鹏先生的书稿——《中华善字经》。书稿独具匠心,取百善之意,一百句,以三字经的形式,语句流畅,层次分明,韵律和美,朗朗上口,宜咏宜吟,令人拍案叫绝。

《中华善字经》是有渊源的。"善乃吉,美之巅"出自东汉许慎《说文解字》:"善,吉也。""善须建,根基坚。善须抱,不脱偏"源自《道德经》:"善建者不拔,善抱者不脱。"凡此种种,《中华善字经》引用大量的古典论述,详尽阐述了"善"的真谛。

《中华善字经》是尊重历史的。它用精练的语言宣扬了历史上"善"的光辉榜样:"华夏善,始轩辕"介绍了"善"的发祥始点;"舜帝善""王祥善"宣扬了"二十四孝"的"孝善";"范蠡善""木兰善"宣扬了中华传统文化中的"义善";孟母的教化之善、孔融的礼仪之善留传至今,影响深远;雷锋、焦裕禄的奉献之善彰显了时代精神,突出榜样的引领作用。

《中华善字经》是紧贴当代的。"为民善,天地宽"道出了激浊扬善的时代主流;"为公善,吏清廉"道出了清廉之源;"为政善,盛世现"表达了人民的心声;"弘扬善,助梦圆"突出了弘扬善文化对实现中国梦具有强大的促进作用。

"人之为善,百善而不足。"善是永绽光芒的精神底色,是不可动摇的道德支柱。"知善、行善、扬善"的使命任重而道远,但只要人人竞相参与,以身践行,源远流长的"善文化"会爆发出前所未有的正能量,让止于至善成为共同的精神追求。

飞鹏先生痴迷于善文化的研究，常常思于脑、润于心、付于行，经过多年的努力，倾心锤炼，方有此上乘佳作。

管子曰："善人者，人亦善之。"善文化的光芒经过历史长河的洗涤，经过智慧星空的启迪，会更加夺目，更加明亮。

（王立群，著名文化学者，河南大学文学院教授、博士生导师、中国古代文学学科带头人，中国《史记》研究会顾问，中国《文选》学会副会长，被观众誉为"百家讲坛最佳学术主讲人"）

A Verse Standing the Trial of Time; a Sutra Extolling Goodness
(Introduction I)

"Goodness", inherent to Chinese civilization, epitomizes the crucial traits and core values in traditional Chinese culture. Hence the publicity and championing of "the Goodness Culture" is a prerequisite for highlighting the zeitgeist and nurturing socialist core values. Meanwhile, goodness, the embodiment of human nature and an individual's attitude to life, is internalized in one's moral qualities and externalized in his words and deeds.

Goodness has played a fundamental role in national governance for all heydays of past dynasties in China. Moreover, the enrichment and promotion of goodness is the cornerstone of the Chinese nation to govern the country or manage a family, thus a full range of family teachings passed on from generation to generation have bloomed into classics.

For instance, *The Yans' Family Teachings*, the first classic among many of its kind, tells us how to implement goodness and manage a family in detail; *The Zhus' Family Teachings*, also a masterwork about family teaching, illustrates how to cultivate one's moral character and run a household successfully. Besides, some famous lines from the book, such as "Goodness to show is not goodness true", are still remembered today.

"Man on earth, / Good at birth", a widely-known motto from ancient times, explains the meaning of goodness, enlightening people with wisdom; "Blessed be he who pursues goodness" is a tenet that has influenced so many generations that regard doing good deeds as a philosophy of life; the proverb "Do not commit it because it is a small sin; do not discard it because it is a small pin" also illuminates to us how to be someone good.

Thousands of years have witnessed the passing-on of goodness that has influenced the Chinese people for ages. Besides, the idea to advocate goodness and do good deeds is the core of the traditional education of the Chinese nation.

The Goodness Culture, the fruits of human culture, may date back to ancient times, growing with human progress. However, it is difficult to extract the pith and express it due to the length of history and the depth of culture. The philosophical radiance and classical exposition of goodness are mostly achievements of the ancients, while nowadays people practice more but explore less of the connotations of goodness, hence fewer systematic and theoretical achievements. Therefore, the era is calling for goodness and classical masterworks about the Goodness Culture.

I feel honored to read the manuscript of *Three-Word Primer of Goodness* by Mr. Yin

Feipeng, a famous calligrapher, in this golden autumn. The ingenious and stunning manuscript comprises a hundred fluent and well-arranged lines, symbolizing an altitude of goodness in simulation of *Three Word Primer*, rhythmic and beautiful, catchy and appropriate to chant.

Many lines of *Three-Word Primer of Goodness* have their origin, such as "Goodness is divine, / Beauty's top sign" from "Goodness is beauty" in *Origin of Chinese Characters* written by Xu Shen in the Eastern Han dynasty. "Goodness we found/ On firm ground. Goodness we hold, / A yardstick gold" comes from *The Word and the World*, and so on. In a word, *Three-Word Primer of Goodness* explicates the true meaning of "goodness" by referring or alluding to many quotations from classics. *Three-Word Primer of Goodness*, based on historical facts, promotes the glorious models of "goodness" in history in concise language: "China's goodness then, / With Cartshaft began" unveils the starting of "goodness"; "Lord Hibiscus good" and "Wang Xiang good" advocate "filial piety" of "24 Examples of Filial Piety"; "Saint Fan good" and "Mulan, then, likewise" promote "righteousness good" in traditional Chinese culture; Mencius's Mum's good education, and Kong Rong's good manners still exert a far-reaching influence today; Lei Feng or Jiao Yulu's good dedication shows the spirit of the time, highlighting the leading influence of role models.

Three-Word Primer of Goodness keeps abreast with the time: "Do people good; / Win you could" embodies the mainstream values of the time which is to eliminate vice and exalt virtue; "Do public good; / Serve you would" stems the source of corruption; "Do governing good; / Prosper we could" expresses the voice of the people; "What's good extolled, / All strike gold" highlights the impetus of the Goodness Culture given to the realization of Chinese Dream.

"A hundred good deeds do not necessarily make a true good man." Goodness, the spiritual undertone with eternal light, has proved to be the backbone of morality. However, there's still a long way to go for the fulfillment of the mission of "Knowing goodness, doing goodness and promoting goodness", but as long as everyone participates and does good deeds, the age-old "Goodness Culture" will give out unprecedented positive energy so that the supreme Goodness becomes our common spiritual pursuit.

Feipeng, fascinated with the study of the Goodness Culture, thinks, learns and acts, and has refined this masterpiece through many years of hard work and dedication. As Guanzi, a legalist in the Spring and Autumn period, said, "Goodness comes both ways." The Goodness Culture is bound to shine in the long course of history and in the starry sky of human wisdom.

Wang Liqun

October, 2017

(Wang Liqun, a famous cultural scholar, professor of School of Literature, PhD supervisor and leader of the study of ancient Chinese literature at Henan University, Consultant of the *Records of the Grand Historian* Society and Vice President of the *Chinese Literature Selection* Society, is commended as the best academic speaker of CCTV *Lecture Hall*.)

逐善——读尹飞鹏《中华善字经》有感
（代序2）

面对尹飞鹏，很难用一句话来界定他的身份。

在家族内，他是血浓于水的核心人；在朋友中，他是豪爽仗义的热心人；在乡亲里，他是反哺故里的善心人；在书法界，他是名闻燕赵的书法家；在篆刻群，他是誉满冀南的篆刻家；在文学圈，他还是小有名气的土作家……

印象中，我与飞鹏兄的初见，于20世纪80年代末期。

那是一个晴朗的中午，我去邯郸市电台拜访同乡好友任和平。在他的办公室里，我见到一个标配的青年，瘦高的身材，茂密的黑发，炯亮的眼睛，说话高声大嗓，行走风风火火，一副青春飞扬的模样。那一天，我们相谈甚欢，无非是些艺术至上、理想无敌之类的时髦话题。澄明的阳光照映着他那红彤彤的脸庞，似乎能听到热血的喧响。和平介绍说，这是同学尹飞鹏，书法家。

忽然想起，在几次书法展览中，我欣赏过他的作品，行云流水，笔墨灵动，一如眼前的他，虽略显青涩，却富有成长性，似乎无所不能。

1962年，飞鹏兄生于成安县城东部的一个村庄，三个弟弟，没有姐妹。这在那个贫寒的年代里，便是父母特殊的苦累了。好在，受父亲影响，他从小喜欢书法，初临柳楷，后习汉隶。虽然懵懵懂懂，却已蹒蹒跚跚。

初中毕业，回家务农，愁云迷雾，不辨前程。时值邯郸招待处招考服务员，他前去应试，竟然得中。这在当时，也是一个美丽的差事。只是，一个小伙子，每天铺床叠被，扫地冲厕，确有诸多尴尬。但在烦琐、枯燥和熏臭之余，他点燃梦想，固执初心，一管孤笔，临摹古韵。青灯孤影寒，瀚墨飘肉香。不仅如此，他还有了"新欢"——篆刻。一方印石，金戈铁马，如痴如醉，春雨杏花。正是花前月下的恋爱季节，外人不堪清冷，他却沉醉其中。

慢慢地，他开始在当地报纸频频发表书法、篆刻作品。一棵幼苗，悄然绽蕾。知识改变命运，恰逢市税务局招考打字员。他，再次得中。

大约1994年，我在报社工作，飞鹏前来造访。几年不见，他已浑厚许多，魁梧且儒雅，沉稳又精悍，宛若树木初夏时的葱茏与繁茂。

的确，这期间他历经了一次次蝶变，先是脱产到高校系统学习，取得正规文凭，而后正式到行政机关从事文字工作。飞鹏似乎对文字有着一种特殊感觉，不仅把公文搞得有声有色，还根据工作生活中的诸多感悟，创作了一系列散文和时评，多有发表，并在全国获奖。

可以说，整个20世纪90年代，是飞鹏书篆创作的探索、飞升期。他将艺术的触角延伸到一个更广领域，把汉简、楚简、章草等书体开辟为新的主战场。工作之余，夜静之时，刀笔在手，聚精会神，揣摩古人的书写之风、构字之意，从古朴浑厚中寻找线条的俊秀与灵动，在苍茫斑驳里禅悟自然与天籁的玄机。从而，将僵直化为柔美，将枯槁化为圆润，将密集化为疏朗，将刻板化为活泼。

进入 21 世纪以来，我基本离开邯郸，在外地创业。虽然与飞鹏联系不多，却也在关注着他的讯息，似乎也在期待着什么。果然，他的艺术进入黄金季节，不仅连连得奖，还加入中国书法家协会，成为公认的书法、篆刻名家。但是，他并没有止步，而是再一次开疆拓土，凝眸于传统文化，特别是中华善文化。他先后到北京大学、南开大学、浙江大学、厦门大学等名校拜师求教，问学善道。为此，他还多次出入国家图书馆，并三次赴西安碑林研究孝经碑，探寻百善之"先"。传统文化的滋润，使他的思考更加高邃。

2014 年秋，我在邯郸参加一个学术研讨会，意外邂逅飞鹏。正值中年的他，体态壮硕，红光满面，神色坚毅，笑声朗朗。他兴致勃勃地向我介绍正在编著的《中华善字经》一书。当时，我有些惊诧和怀疑，中国善文化悠远精深，抽象宽泛，不易归纳，难以表达，于是，便委婉且真诚地流露了一种消极情绪。

不想，飞鹏并没有畏难，而是继续前进。更让我意外的是，飞鹏兄不仅痴迷于善文化的追根溯源，还热心于亲身践行。他是有名的热心肠，朋友有难，尽力支援；父老乡亲进城看病，他主动联系医院，垫付药费；近年来，他先后资助 7 个贫困孩子，帮助完成大学学业；逢节假日，他常常回到村里，举办书法培训；每年春节，他都要组织市里的书法家朋友为全村义务书写对联。于是，3 800 余人的村庄，竟然有近千人热爱书法，被河北省书法家协会命名为全省第一批书法示范村。

外界一片和善，家庭更是美善。他的老母亲，八十有余，依然康健，逢人便说："我们这个大家庭，兄弟间从无矛盾，妯娌间情同姊妹，全凭飞鹏这个带头大哥。"

哦，是什么力量，使他如此呢？从艺术的大美，走向生命的大善。

"善"，会意字，从羊从言，本义是像羊一样说话。像羊一样说话，才不会吵架、打架，即使打架也不会伤害对方，因为羊最大的特点是犄角内弯。所以，羊是中华民族最初始的吉祥物，善是传统文化最深蕴的潜意识。任继愈在《中国哲学史》中明言：合规律发展的"欲"，就是善。而西方哲学也定义：在最广时间范围内符合最大多数人的目的，即为善。

的确，艺术之美的极致，天地人心的极致，文明发展的极致，皆为善。

因此，作为艺术家的飞鹏，敏感地、真挚地、彻底地理解了善，融入了善，拥抱了善，进而化身于善。

今年9月的一个傍晚，秋风涂金，熟果飘香，我与飞鹏、和平二兄又相聚一起。

和平兄苍然白发，已从市电台副台长任上卸职；飞鹏兄呢，亦是满头稀疏，脸颊黑黄，步履沉重。当年那个高高瘦瘦、神采飞扬的小伙子，早已褪去青春的衣衫，变成一个富态厚重的"奔六"之人了。时光的珍珠，意念的灵芝，梦想的沉浮，精神的舍利，改变着也定格着内心和身外的世界，亦如飞鹏兄的书法和篆刻，由绚烂至极复归平淡质朴，化作一纸苍茫、一方宁静。

临别之时，飞鹏拿出一卷书稿，请我审阅。原来，他精心推敲多年的《中华善字经》，即将付梓。

回到家里，燃灯细观。综览全书，内心惊叹。全书共一百句，取百善之意，分上下两篇。上篇为理论，告诉人们"善是什么"；下篇为践行，告诉人们"如何行善"。文本上借鉴《三字经》，三字一句，结构严谨，韵律和谐，朗朗上口。在内容上，则又引经据典，条分缕析，娓娓道来，寓教于乐，不仅对中国传统善文化进行系统梳理，而且对接当今，突出现实。

善乃天地之心，无形无影，抽象玄妙，要写出它的形象性、立体性、鲜明性、深刻性、精妙性与实用性，殊为不易。而他，倾一人之力，聚数年之功，集百善之句，述千年善道，把善的筋骨、善的血肉、善的风韵、善的明眸、善的芳香，体会和提炼得如此绘声绘色，秋毫毕现，雅俗共赏，入目入心，实乃生命之作也。

如此善"经"，非常人擅自可为也。很多哲人想梳理，有思想却没有实践；好多善者想总结，有实践却亏欠理性；好多文人想概括，有理性却缺少体悟。文人做不了它，哲人做不了它，官人做不了它，商人做不了它，俗人更做不了它。只有像他这样，亦官亦民、亦雅亦俗、亦正亦野之人，才能为之。

善念善心，善举善行。知善致善，是为上善。瓜熟蒂落，方有善果。

总之，此书出自飞鹏，适得其人，舍他其谁？白驹过隙，逝者如斯，繁华散尽，美善归一。未来三五年，飞鹏兄必将退休。但书法家的他，治印家的他，善文化学者的他，永远不会休退。

值此大著出版之际，身为老乡兼老友，我只有祝贺。祝贺大美大善，祝贺善美永恒，祝贺善义有邻，祝贺善有善报。

特为善者序！

李春雷
2017.7.19

（李春雷，著名作家、鲁迅文学奖获得者，中国报告文学学会副会长，河北省作家协会副主席）

Pursuing Goodness
—Reflections on *Three-Word Primer of Goodness* by Yin Feipeng
(Introduction II)

Yin Feipeng's identity is hard to define.

As a core member in his family, he cherishes kinship more than anything else, and as a friend, he is a warm-hearted companion with generosity and righteousness; in the eyes of his fellow men, he is a good-hearted villager returning grace to his hometown; in calligraphy circles, he is a well-known calligraphist throughout Hebei Province; in the field of seal cutting, he is a well-reputed seal-cutter all over Southern Hebei; in literary circles, he is a folk writer who has gained some reputation.

In my memory, Feipeng and I first met in the late 1980s.

It was a sunny noon; I called on my fellow townsman and good friend, Ren Heping, at Handan Radio Station. There in his office I noticed a lean and tall young man, with sparkling eyes and thick black hair. He talked sonorously and walked vigorously, radiating the energy of a promising young man.

    That day, we had a wonderful chat at random on such *avant-garde* topics as supremacy of art, invincibility of ideals and so on. I could still recall the clear sunlight reflected on his glowing red face, as if the ardor in his vein were boiling. My friend Heping moved to us and formally introduced to me the young man, who was his classmate Yin Feipeng, a calligraphist.

    Suddenly it occurred to me that his lifelike works, which I had appreciated during several calligraphic exhibitions, seemed so natural, like floating clouds and flowing water, just like himself in front of me, slightly inexperienced, but full of energy as if omnipotent.

    Feipeng was born in a village in the east of Cheng'an County in 1962, having three younger brothers but no sister, which meant special hardship for his parents at that time. Fortunately, under his father's influence, he fell to calligraphy in his childhood. In the primary stage, he first learned Liu's style, the standard script of calligraphy, and then advanced to Han script of calligraphy. He felt muddled in the beginning, but managed to toddle through the interior of calligraphy.

    He went back home for farming after graduating from a junior high school, lost and worried, and just at that time Handan Hotel happened to recruit attendants, therefore he went to interview. Unexpectedly, he got a job, which was a good errand at that time. However, this did embarrass a young man a lot to make bed, sweep the floor and clean bathrooms every day. Somehow, after the tedious, boring and stinking work hours, he lit his dream with a persistent heart, facsimileing ancient calligraphy with an ink brush, lonely but wholeheartedly.

    The blue lamp casts a cold shadow, while fragrance of the ink does float. Besides, he got a "new lover"—seal cutting. Holding a piece of seal stone, like a cavalryman swaying a gold spear, he was obsessed and lost in his dreams, where prunus trees bloomed in a spring rain. It was a season that lovers would date before the flowers and under the moon, while he was crazily immersed in his own world, sipping and enjoying the loneliness that others could hardly bear.

Gradually, his calligraphic and seal cutting works were frequently published on local newspapers. A seedling was quietly blooming. As the saying goes, knowledge changes destiny; he seized the opportunity again when the municipal tax bureau recruited typists.

In about 1994, Feipeng came to visit me when I was working at a newspaper agency. After a couple of years, he had been a lot more sturdy, stalwart and graceful, steady and intrepid, like a verdant and luxuriant tree in early summer.

Indeed, he has experienced a butterfly-like metamorphosis these years, during which he firstly took a full-time course in the university systematically and obtained a formal diploma, then worked on writing formally in an administrative organ. Feipeng seems to be gifted, a special talent of words, not only capable of writing formal official documents, but also creating a series of prose and news commentaries based on the wealth of thoughts sparked in his work and daily life. Furthermore, most of his creations were published, and even won national prizes.

So to say, the whole 1990s witnessed the exploring and soaring of Feipeng's calligraphy and seal-cutting. He even extended the tentacles of art to a wider realm, opening up new battlefields like bamboo-slip calligraphy popular in the periods of Chu and Han more than two thousand years ago, and memorial scripts of calligraphy (a type of cursive script that evolved in the Han dynasty). After work, when everything was silently bathing in pale moonlight, he would be absorbed in the style of ancients' handwriting and character formation, with a carving knife and ink brush in hand, looking for the delicate and lively beauty of the strokes through the classic characters, to unveil the mystery of the nature through these mottled seal-cuttings, thus undergoing a process from stiff to soft, withered to mellow, dense to sparse, rigid to lively.

At the turning point of the 21st century, I left Handan to start a business. Although we had not contacted a lot, I still cared about him, looking forward to hearing something good about him. As expected, he had entered his golden season, not only winning awards from time to time, but also winning fame as a well-acknowledged calligraphist after joining the Chinese Calligraphists' Association. However, he did not stop there, but once again rose to open up new territories, focusing his eyes on traditional culture, especially the Goodness Culture. For this reason, he went to Peking University, Nankai University, Zhejiang University, Xiamen University and some famous schools for advice and lessons of goodness from great masters. Besides, he went to the National Library several times, and three times to Xi'an Forest of Gravestones to study filial classics, exploring the "foundation" with a hundred examples of goodness. In turn, traditional culture also nourishes his thinking into a deeper realm.

In autumn 2014, I attended an academic seminar in Handan and came across Feipeng, middle-aged, robust with a firm expression and clarion laughter. In high spirits, he introduced me to the book *Three-Word Primer of Goodness*, which was being composed then. I was a little bit surprised and suspicious at that time, because the Goodness Culture is not easy to embody or express due to its abstraction and profoundness, so I declined with a negative emotion about it tactfully and sincerely.

However, Feipeng continued to forge ahead without fear. Furthermore, he was not only obsessed with the origin of the Goodness Culture, but also eager to do good deeds. As a well-known warm-hearted person, he always tried his best to help when friends were in difficulty; whenever his fellow-villagers came downtown to see a doctor, he would take the initiative to contact the hospital and paid for medicines; in recent years, he has sponsored seven children in need successively to help them finish their college education; every holiday, he would return to the village for calligraphy training; every spring festival, he would organize his calligraphist friends to write couplets for the village. Thanks to him, the village has nearly 1,000 calligraphy-lovers out of 3,800 villagers, and has been named the province's First Village of Calligraphy Demonstration by Hebei Calligraphists' Association.

Outside, the world is in good harmony, and inside, his family is even more blessed. His old mother, in her 80s, is still in good health and to everyone she would say: "It is to Feipeng, the eldest brother, that we owe the great harmony among brothers and sisters-in-law. He is indeed the best lubricant of our big family."

Oh, what power has rendered him so? Marching from the great beauty of art to the great goodness of life.

"Goodness", the word with many associations, originally means speaking like sheep in a way that is not quarrelsome, for the reason that the biggest characteristic of the sheep is to introvert their horns; even if they fight, they will not hurt each other. The sheep symbolizes the original mascot of the Chinese nation; therefore the goodness lies in the profoundest subconsciousness of traditional culture. As the historian and philosopher Ren Jiyu says in *The*

History of Chinese Philosophy, the "desire" that follows the course of natural laws can be called goodness. Western philosophy also defines goodness as what is in line with most people's interests in the broadest range of time and space.

Indeed, the supreme beauty of art, the supreme of people's heart, heaven and earth and the development of civilization are all goodness.

Therefore, as an artist, Feipeng comprehends the goodness thoroughly, sensitively and sincerely, embracing, integrating, and incarnating all elements in the sainthood of goodness.

One evening in September this year, when autumn wind painted everything gold and ripe fruits released pleasant fragrance, Feipeng, Heping and I had a reunion again.

Heping, hoary-headed, has retired from the position of deputy director of the radio station; Feipeng, plodding heavily, was an image of sparse hair and dark-yellow cheeks. That slender and vigorous young man has taken off the clothes of youth for long and become a portly man in his late fifties. The internal mind and external world have been changed and frozen by the pearl of time, the glossy ganoderma of mind, the ups and downs of dream, and the Buddhist sarira of spirit, and likewise Feipeng's calligraphy and seal cuttings have also changed from splendid and gorgeous to plain and simple, finally turning into a piece of boundlessness, a piece of serenity.

When we were about to part, Feipeng took out a volume of manuscript and invited me to review it. It turned out that the *Three-Word Primer of Goodness* he had carefully studied for many years would soon go to press.

Back home, I turned on the light and looked through the book carefully. I was so amazed by the book, which comprises two parts and a hundred lines, symbolizing a hundred cases of goodness. The former part is something like theories of goodness, telling people "what goodness is"; the latter part is practices of goodness, guiding people "how to do good deeds". In terms of the structure, the text comprises a hundred fluent and well-balanced lines, symbolizing a hundred cases of goodness and sharing the same form with *Three Word Primer*, rhythmic and beautiful, catchy and appropriate to chant. In terms of the content, it is pearled with quotations from classics with detailed annotations, and enlightens people with pleasure and kindly narration, not only arranging the traditional Chinese Goodness Culture systematically, but also highlighting the reality nowadays, in line with the trend of the age.

Goodness epitomizes the heart of heaven and earth, intangible and invisible, abstract and mysterious, so it is really not easy to write out its image, its three-dimensional, vivid, profound, subtle and practical nature. However, with all Feipeng's dedication and a couple of years' hard work, he has comprehended and extracted the flesh and blood, clear eyes, charm and fragrance of Chinese goodness so vividly and concretely, to tell a tale of the Goodness Culture with a thousand years of history through a hundred lines, not only catchy and touching, but also suiting both high-brow and popular tastes.

None but an extraordinary person is able to work on such a Goodness "Sutra". Many philosophers have thoughts but no practices even if they want to organize it; many philanthropists take to practices but lack rational thoughts even if they want to conclude it; scholars have got rational thoughts but lack experiences even if they want to generalize it, thus no scholars, philosophers, officials or merchants can do it, let alone common people, but a man like him, an official as well as a citizen, elegant and ordinary, decent and rustic, could do it well.

Good thoughts come from good hearts, breeding good deeds and actions. To know goodness and to do good deeds are the supreme goodness, furthermore, there will be tasty fruits when the melons of goodness are ripe.

In a word, this book is written by Feipeng, the best choice of the time. The prosperity will fade away as time goes by; the goodness and beauty will unite in the twinkling of an eye. In the next three or five years, Feipeng will retire from work, but as a calligraphist, engraver and scholar of the Goodness Culture, he will never retire.

At the time when this masterpiece is ready to go to press, as a fellow-townsman and an old friend, I just want to give my sincere congratulations to him. May great beauty and goodness go eternal, may goodness and righteousness go in pairs, and may it be good karma!

Especially, this introduction is for the good!

Li Chunlei

July 19th, 2017

(Li Chunlei, a famous writer, winner of Lu Xun Literature Award, Vice President of Chinese Society of Reportage, Vice President of Hebei Writers' Association)

上篇
Part I

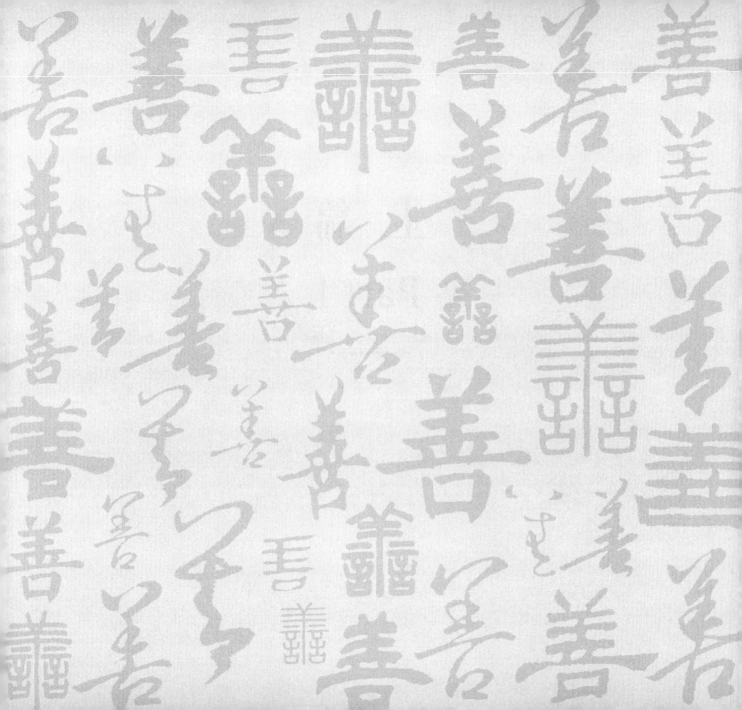

Three-Word Primer of Goodness
(Chinese–English Bilingual Edition)

shàn nǎi xìng　　tiān dì jiàn
善乃性①，天地见。

shàn dāng xiān　　kāi zōng yuán
善当先，开宗元。

Goodness is nature,②

As Heavens nurture.

Goodness does run

Before the One③.

◎ 本书用汉语拼音字母给经文原文的每个单字注音，不按词连写；注原调，不注变调，如："不"均作 bù 。

Part I

【释义 / Paraphrase】

　　善是人之天性，这种天性天地可见证。把善放在首位，是做人谋事、开宗明义的先决条件。

　　Goodness is the nature of mankind, which is determined by Heavens. One should put goodness in the first place before he decides how to behave and how to do things.

【注释 / Notes】

　　① 《三字经》："人之初，性本善。"意思是人生下来的时候，本性都是好的。

　　② Goodness is nature: as *Three-Word Primer* says, "Man on earth, / Good at birth. The same nature/ Varies on nurture." When one is born, he is naturally good.

　　③ the One: the beginning of all things.

Three-Word Primer of Goodness
(Chinese-English Bilingual Edition)

shàn wéi běn lì shì jiān
善为本①，立世间。

shàn wéi mài shì dài chuán
善为脉，世代传。

Goodness, the base②,

For every race.

Goodness, the vein,

All ages' gain.

Part I

【释义 / Paraphrase】

善是做人的根本，与人为善，和谐相处，才能屹立于世间。善是中华民族传统文化的根脉，世代相传，生生不息。

Goodness is the prerequisite of being human. Only if one shows goodness to others and gets along well with others can he be a man. Goodness is a Chinese vein and has been passed on from generation to generation.

【注释 / Notes】

①本，这里指事物的根源，与末相对。"人性本善"是儒家的最基本观点。"以善为本"就是劝诫人们要以善作为人性之本，多行善，不能摒弃善良的本性。

② the base: the foundation for all things. Goodness or goodness of human nature is an important Confucian notion.

<ruby>善<rt>shàn</rt></ruby><ruby>乃<rt>nǎi</rt></ruby><ruby>吉<rt>jí</rt></ruby>①，<ruby>美<rt>měi</rt></ruby><ruby>之<rt>zhī</rt></ruby><ruby>巅<rt>diān</rt></ruby>。
<ruby>善<rt>shàn</rt></ruby><ruby>源<rt>yuán</rt></ruby><ruby>悯<rt>mǐn</rt></ruby>，<ruby>发<rt>fā</rt></ruby><ruby>于<rt>yú</rt></ruby><ruby>怜<rt>lián</rt></ruby>。

Goodness is divine,②

Beauty's top sign.

Goodness is love,

With mercy above.

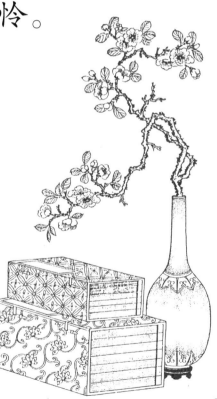

【释义 / Paraphrase】

　　善的本义是吉祥，美是善的象征，善是美的最高境界。善来源于关爱同情之心，生发于怜爱之意。

　　"Good" derives from "god", an old word divine, meaning "excellent" and "fine". Beauty is a representative of goodness and goodness is supreme beauty. Goodness comes from a merciful heart and develops into love.

【注释 / Notes】

　　①善，会意字，从羊从言。本义是"吉祥"。东汉·许慎《说文解字》："善，吉也。"

　　② Goodness comes from God, so it is divine.

善须建，根基坚。

善须抱，不脱偏。①

Goodness we found

On firm ground.②

Goodness we hold,

A yardstick gold.

【释义 / Paraphrase】

注重自身道德修养的人，做人的根基才能牢固。始终坚持以善为念，做人的目标才不会偏离方向。

He who keeps cultivating a sense of goodness has a solid ground for being human; he who sticks to being good will not feel lost.

【注释 / Notes】

①《道德经》："善建者不拔，善抱者不脱。"建，制定合乎自身的道德规范。抱，秉持自己所认识到的道德准则。善于制定合乎自身道德规范的人，是坚决不会动摇的；善于秉持自己道德准则的人，是不会丧失自信的。

② A verse in *The Word and the World* by Laocius reads like this: "He who knows how to settle himself does not break off; he who knows how to conserve himself does not drop off." To settle oneself means one needs a firm ground.

<ruby>善<rt>shàn</rt></ruby><ruby>者<rt>zhě</rt></ruby><ruby>学<rt>xué</rt></ruby>，<ruby>纳<rt>nà</rt></ruby><ruby>百<rt>bǎi</rt></ruby><ruby>川<rt>chuān</rt></ruby>①。

<ruby>善<rt>shàn</rt></ruby><ruby>者<rt>zhě</rt></ruby><ruby>思<rt>sī</rt></ruby>②，<ruby>意<rt>yì</rt></ruby><ruby>高<rt>gāo</rt></ruby><ruby>瞻<rt>zhān</rt></ruby>。

The good learn

Never to spurn.③

The good look

Over every nook.④

【释义 / Paraphrase】

　　善良的人虚心好学，博采众长，善于借鉴别人的经验，吸取知识就像海纳百川。善良的人为人处事都会从善的角度去思考问题，遇事才能高瞻远瞩，正确抉择。

　　A good person is modest and studious. He learns widely from others' strong points, draws on others' experience and absorbs knowledge as if the sea welcomes all rivers. A good person thinks and behaves based on goodness so that he will have a broad, long-term view and make right decisions.

【注释 / Notes】

　　①晋·袁宏《三国名臣序赞》："形器不存，方寸海纳。"唐·李周翰注："方寸之心，如海之纳百川也，言其包含广也。"比喻包容的东西非常广泛，而且数量很大。明·方正学《赠俞子严溪喻》："善学者，其如海乎。"

　　②曾子在《论语·学而》中说："吾日三省吾身，为人谋而不忠乎？"意思是"我每天多次反省自己，替人家谋事是否不够尽心"。儒家强调通过自我反思来保持心灵的平衡。

　　③ The good learn/ Never to spurn: A good person receives advice like a sea receiving all rivers.

　　④ The good look/ Over every nook: Tsengcius said, "I have three introspections a day: Am I not loyal to others? Am I not faithful with friends? Am I slack in my school work?"

^{shàn zhě xiū} ^{dé zhāng xiǎn}
善者修，德彰显。

^{shàn zhě xíng} ^{pǐn zhì duān}
善者行，品质端。

The good build,

Hence virtue revealed.

The good act,

Hence quality intact.

【释义 / Paraphrase】

善良的人注重自身修为，道德素养才能不断提高，其崇高的品德令人敬仰。善良的人常怀慈爱之心、常行善义之举，才能胸怀坦荡、品行端正。

A good man keeps cultivating his mind to improve his moral accomplishment, and he will be respected for his virtue. A good man, with a kind heart and good deeds, has an open mind and good qualities.

shàn qí shēn, dá zé jiān。①
善其身，达则兼。
shàn qí jiā, fú shòu quán
善其家，福寿全。

Goodness perfects one

And benefits everyone.②

Goodness perfects you;

Your family grow.

【释义 / Paraphrase】

　　人要洁身自好，努力提高个人修养，才能成就一番事业，造福百姓。把善作为教育子孙立身处世、持家治业的根本，家庭才能美满幸福，家人才能快乐安康。

　　One should preserve his moral integrity and improve his qualities so as to achieve great success and benefit others. When goodness is regarded as the foundation of educating later generations about how to conduct, the family will live in peace and love.

【注释 / Notes】

　　①《孟子·尽心上》："穷则独善其身，达则兼善天下。"意思是不得志的时候就要注重自己的道德修养，得志的时候就要努力让百姓都能得到好处。

　　② Mencius said, "Unfavored, I perfect myself; established, I better the world."

shàn zhī shǒu　　xiào wéi xiān
善之首，孝为先。
shàn zhī chéng　　qīng chū lán
善之承，青出蓝。

Goodness should lead

A pious deed.

Goodness should guide

A better pride.

【释义 / Paraphrase】

"百善孝为先",对父母长辈的孝顺和恭敬应放在首位。善在不断传承,经久不衰,一代胜于一代。

Filial piety comes to the fore out of all virtues. As goodness is passed on, it will never cease to get more influential from generation to generation.

^{shàn yǒu gēn}
善有根①，^{zhī yè fán}枝叶繁。

^{shàn yǒu guǒ}
善有果②，^{yǔ yīn lián}与因连。

Goodness can raise

Good lush sprays.

Goodness now fruits[3]

With good roots[4].

【释义 / Paraphrase】

善像大树的根一样，根深才能枝繁叶茂。善是有果的，这种果是与善因相连的，种什么因结什么果。

Goodness is like the roots of a tree. Only deep roots can raise lush branches and leaves. Roots and fruits are cause and effect—good roots bring about good fruits.

【注释 / Notes】

①佛学有三善根：无贪善根、无嗔善根和无痴善根。

②果，事情的结局或成效。

③ fruits: effect or efficacy.

④ Three good roots in Buddhism: no greed, no anger, no infatuation.

^{shàn yǒu bào} ^{yīng xiāng yàn}
善有报①，应相验②。
^{shàn yǒu héng} ^{mò děng xián}
善有恒，莫等闲。

Goodness is repaid,③

A testament made.④

Goodness lasts long;

Act while young.

【释义 / Paraphrase】

　　古人曰："积善即积福。"助人为乐，多行善举，经常帮助别人，一定会得到好的回报。行善贵在持之以恒，主动作为，不要等将来才后悔。

　　As an old saying goes, "Doing good brings up good fortune." One will get repaid if he often gives a hand to others. The importance of doing good lies in perseverance and taking initiatives. Do not hesitate to do good at present, or one may regret in the future.

【注释 / Notes】

　　①《名贤集》："积善有善报，积恶有恶报。"宋·李昌龄《太上感应篇》："善恶之报，如影随形。"

　　②佛教中因果报应，指事物的起因和结果，种什么因，结什么果。

　　③ Good is repaid with good, and evil with evil.

　　④ As is termed in Buddhist karma, what goes around, comes around.

^{shàn yì shuō}   ^{xíng què nán}
善 易 说， 行 却 难。①

^{shàn wéi niàn}   ^{cháng zì miǎn}
善 为 念②， 常 自 勉③。

Goodness, easier said

Than done instead.④

Goodness in mind,

Never lag behind.⑤

【释义 / Paraphrase】

天下事，不在难知，而在难行，善说起来容易，能事事以善为念并付诸行动却不容易。要把做一个正直善良的人作为人生信念，始终牢记在心上，时常勉励自己为善最乐。

What is difficult lies in action instead of knowing. Goodness is easy to say, but not easy to put into practice. One should be firm on keeping goodness as his belief, keeping it in mind and exhort himself to do good.

【注释 / Notes】

①知易行难，出自《尚书·商书·说命中》。原文："非知之艰，行之惟艰。"知易行难指认识事物的道理较易，实行其事较难；明白认知善的道理是一回事，是否能做到做好又是另外一回事。

②南朝·梁·萧纲《唱导文》："故一善染心，万劫不朽。百灯旷照，千里通明。"

③《庄子·天运》："此皆自勉，以役其德者也。"

④ It's easier said than done. To know what is goodness is easy, but to do good is not as easy.

⑤ Goodness in mind, / Never lag behind: as is said in *Sir Lush*, "These are but for self-exhortation."

shàn è fēn, shǒu dǐ xiàn
善恶分，守底线。

shàn bù yàn, shī bù juàn
善不厌，施不倦。

Goodness or sin,

Baseline kept therein.

Goodness run e'er;

Give and share.

【释义 / Paraphrase】

善与恶两重天，泾渭分明，界限清晰，要时刻坚守做人的底线。积德行善永不满足，施舍救济永不厌倦。

The boundary between goodness and sin is always clear, so one should always have the baseline in mind. Never feel too contented to do good, and never feel weary of giving and sharing.

shàn shì chǐ　liáng cháng duǎn
善是尺，量长短。
shàn shì fēng　yào dēng pān
善是峰，要登攀。

Goodness, a rule,

A measuring tool.

Goodness, a peak,

Climb to seek.

【释义 / Paraphrase】

善是一把尺子,能丈量出人间真情,也能反映出社会风尚。善是一座山峰,要努力登攀,登高望远才能领悟善的意境和价值。

Goodness is a rule or ruler. As a ruler, it can be used to measure a real situation and social condition. Goodness, as a peak, requires people to climb high to seek its view and value.

shàn shì qí　　dé xíng zhǎn
善是旗，德行展。
shàn shì rén①　ài wú biān
善是仁①，爱无边。

Goodness, a flag,

Lest virtues sag.

Goodness, love sound②,

Love without bound.

【释义 / Paraphrase】

善是一面旗帜,能展示出时代的主旋律,彰显出高尚的品德。善是仁爱,始终怀着一颗仁爱之心去对待世间万物,才能大爱无垠。

Goodness, as a flag, is a sign for nobility and virtue in this era. Goodness is love, which requires people to treat all things with love so that love will spread beyond bounds.

【注释 / Notes】

①仁,一种道德范畴,指人与人相互友爱、互助、同情等。

② Humanity is an important notion of virtue in the Confucian doctrine—that is love, mutual help and sympathy.

shàn wéi yì, gèn wú xiàn
善为义，亘无限。

shàn wéi lǐ, lì qì liǎn
善为礼，戾气敛。

Goodness, the right,

Reaches the height.

Goodness, the polite,

Sets temper alright.

【释义 / Paraphrase】

善是义，有着无限的正能量，亘古不变。善是礼仪，能够使戾气得以收敛，和顺待人。

Goodness is righteousness that has unlimited power without any change in time and space; goodness is a rite that can rein your anger and make you treat others with good manner.

shàn wéi zhì　　míng zhě xián
善为智，明者贤。

shàn wéi xìn　　rén zì ān
善为信，人自安。

Goodness, the wise,

Clear sagacious eyes.

Goodness, a creed,

All settle indeed.

【释义 / Paraphrase】

善是一种智慧，一种精神力量，古来圣贤都因善良而使自己更加贤明。善是诚信的核心，对人守信、对事负责的人，胸怀坦荡，安然自得。

Goodness is a kind of wisdom, a spiritual power. Sages become more sagacious because of goodness. Goodness is the core of honesty. An honest and responsible man would be open-minded and feel at ease.

<pre>
shàn ruò jīn   nài huǒ liàn
善若金，耐火炼。
shàn ruò mù   xuě zhōng tàn
善若木，雪中炭。
</pre>

Goodness, like gold,

Hot or cold!

Goodness, like wood,

Fire and food.

【释义 / Paraphrase】

善像永不变色的金子,耐得住烈火的冶炼。善像燃烧的木炭,能给大雪中受寒的人带来温暖。

Goodness is like gold, smelted in fire, but its color is unchanged. Goodness, like a burning charcoal, brings warmth against a blizzard.

shàn ruò shuǐ　　zé huāng yuán
善若水，泽荒原。

shàn ruò tǔ　　wàn wù fán
善若土，万物蕃。

Goodness, like water,

Flows far, farther.

Goodness, like earth,

Gives all worth.

【释义 / Paraphrase】

善像清澈的泉水,能够泽润荒原,带来生机。善像孕物的沃土,滋养万物生长,繁茂不绝。

Goodness, like clear water, nourishes a barren field and brings vigor. Goodness is like fertile soil, in which life flourishes and prospers.

_{shàn} _{rú} _{rì}　　_{míng} _{yǔ} _{huán}
善如日，明宇寰。
_{shàn} _{rú} _{yuè}　　_{yǐng} _{bù} _{dān}
善如月，影不单①。

Goodness, the sun,

Cosmos well shone.

Goodness, the moon,

You, not alone.②

【释义 / Paraphrase】

　　善就像光芒四射的太阳一样，能够给人间带来光明。善就像皓月一样照亮夜空，使人在夜晚不感到孤单。

　　Goodness, like the glowing sun, brings brightness to the world; goodness, like the bright moon, lightens the night sky and dispels one's loneliness.

【注释 / Notes】

　　①唐·李白《月下独酌》："举杯邀明月，对影成三人。"

　　② Goodness, the moon, / You, not alone: Li Bai's lines read like this: "My cup raised, I invite the moon, / With my shadow, three for the boon."

_{shàn rú xīng   xiàn cuǐ càn}
善如星，献璀璨。

_{shàn rú chén   qū hēi àn}
善如辰，驱黑暗。

Goodness, the star,

Bright you are.

Goodness, the blue,

All darkness go.

【释义 / Paraphrase】

善就像天上的点点繁星，相互映照，在夜空中闪耀着光芒。善就像辰光一样，能够驱走黑暗，照亮人间。

Goodness, like stars, sparkles with brightness in the night sky; goodness, like the first light of dawn, expels darkness and shines to all.

shàn yì gē　　dòng xīn xián
善亦歌，动心弦。

shàn yì qǔ　　jiě yōu fán
善亦曲，解忧烦。

Goodness you sing,

Moved your heartstring.

Goodness you trill,

All worries kill.

【释义 / Paraphrase】

　　善就像悠扬的歌声一样,能够拨动人们的心弦。善就像美妙的乐曲一样,能够消除人们的忧虑和烦恼。

　　Goodness is like a melodious song that can move one's heartstrings; goodness is like a beautiful melody that can release worry and anxiety.

shàn yì shī　yùn shān lán
善亦诗，韵山岚。

shàn yì huà　huì cháng juàn
善亦画，绘长卷。

Goodness you write,

A poetic sight.

Goodness you paint,

A scroll gained.

【释义 / Paraphrase】

善就像优美的诗句一样，陶冶情操，韵染山岚。善就像一幅唯美的画作，描绘出善行善举的历史长卷。

Goodness, like a beautiful poem, cultivates your sentiment to appreciate nature. Goodness is aesthetic, like a painting depicting good deeds in human history.

<pre>
shàn sì méi   xuě zhōng yàn
善似梅，雪中艳。
shàn sì lán   yōu xiāng dàn
善似兰，幽香淡。
</pre>

Goodness, a wintersweet,

Does snow greet.

Goodness, an orchid,

Sets everything lucid.

【释义 / Paraphrase】

　　善就像蜡梅一样，不畏严寒，在雪中分外鲜艳。善就像深谷幽兰一样，清香淡雅，沁人心脾。

　　Goodness is like a wintersweet, blooming in ice and snow. Goodness is like an orchid in a deep quiet valley with a waft of soothing fragrance.

shàn sì zhú　　jié bù wān
善似竹，节不弯。

shàn sì jú　　yíng shuāng zhàn
善似菊，迎霜绽。

Goodness, a bamboo,

Upright and true.

Goodness, a daisy,

Blows frost dizzy.

【释义 / Paraphrase】

　　善就像生机勃勃的翠竹一样,高风亮节,挺拔向上,宁折不弯。善就像深秋的菊花一样,顶着秋霜,迎风绽放。

　　Goodness, like a lively bamboo, stands upright and unyielding; goodness, like a daisy in late autumn, thrives against frost and wind.

shàn shì jìng　　zhōng jiān biàn
善是镜①，忠奸辨。

shàn shì shǐ　　xīng shuāi jiàn
善是史，兴衰鉴。

Goodness, a mirror②,

Follower or traitor!

Goodness, a history,

A meandering story.

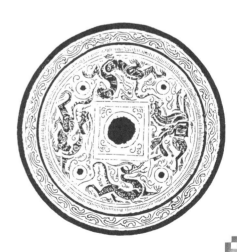

【释义 / Paraphrase】

善如纤毫毕现的镜子，使人们能够辨别是非忠奸。善如浩瀚的史册，人们可从兴衰中吸取经验教训。

Goodness is like a mirror, distinguishing right from wrong, loyalty from betrayal; goodness is like a vast volume of annals, giving lessons of rise and fall.

【注释 / Notes】

①镜鉴：照镜子。《旧唐书·魏徵传》："以铜为镜，可以正衣冠；以古为镜，可以知兴替；以人为镜，可以明得失。"照镜子，不论对照别人，还是对比历史，都能起到借鉴的作用。

② Mirror has been frequently used as a metaphor in Chinese culture. As Wei Zheng, a premier in the Tang dynasty, said, the bronze as a mirror, one can look at himself; the age as a mirror, one can know rise and fall; people as a mirror, one can know gains and pains.

下 篇
Part II

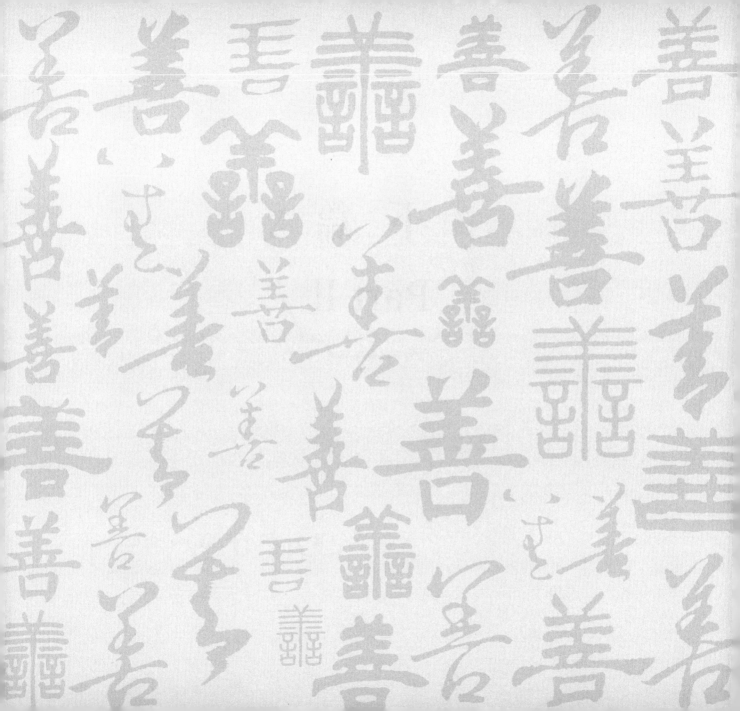

huá xià shàn　　shǐ xuān yuán①
华夏善，始轩辕①。

jì chéng shàn　　xīn huǒ yán
继承善，薪火延。

China's goodness then

With Cartshaft② began.

Goodness passed on

Does endlessly run.

【释义 / Paraphrase】

　　中华民族勤劳善良,华夏文明历史悠久,始于轩辕黄帝。善是中华民族的传统美德,千百年来代代传承,源远流长。

　　China began its civilization and good tradition of hardworking from Cartshaft. Goodness is a Chinese traditional virtue, passed on for thousands of years from generation to generation.

【注释 / Notes】

　　①轩辕是中国远古时代华夏民族的共主,五帝之首,被尊称为中华"人文初祖"。史载轩辕帝因有土德之瑞,故号黄帝。黄帝在位期间,播百谷草木,大力发展生产,始制衣冠、建舟车、制音律、创医学等,得到了民众的爱戴。

　　② Cartshaft: alias Lord Yellow, the first of the five prehistoric lords of China.

shùn dì shàn, xiào gǎn tiān。①
舜帝善，孝感天。

fàn lǐ shàn, qiān jīn sàn。②
范蠡善，千金散。

Lord Hibiscus③ good,

Deeply moved God.

Saint Fan④ good,

Offered all food.

【释义 / Paraphrase】

相传舜帝的父亲和继母曾多次想害死他，舜帝毫不记恨，仍对父母恭顺，他的孝行感动了上天。春秋时期的范蠡多行善举，三散家财施舍给需要帮助的人。

Legend has it that Lord Hibiscus's father and stepmother tried many times to murder him but Lord Hibiscus still treated them with respect and filial piety, whose behaviour moved God. Saint Fan in the Spring and Autumn period was benevolent, offering his wealth to those who needed help.

【注释 / Notes】

①舜，传说中的远古帝王。相传舜在 20 岁的时候以孝行而闻名，因为能对虐待、迫害他的父母坚守孝道，故在青年时代即为人称赞。后尧向四岳（四方诸侯之长）征询继任人选，四岳就推荐了舜。其孝行被后人编为二十四孝之首。

②范蠡，春秋时期楚国人，春秋末著名的政治家、军事家、经济学家和道家学者，他三次经商成巨富，三散家财救济穷人。世人誉之："忠以为国；智以保身；商以致富，成名天下。"

③ Hibiscus: Shun if transliterated, an ancient sovereign, a descendant of Lord Yellow, regarded as one of Five Lords in prehistoric China.

④ Saint Fan: referring to Fan Li (536B.C.-448B.C.), a politician, militarist, economist and Wordist in the later years of the Spring and Autumn period, who helped Goujian, the king of Yue, restore his country.

mèng mǔ shàn　　jū sān qiān

孟母善，居三迁。①

kǒng róng shàn　　yòu zhī qiān

孔融善，幼知谦。②

Mencius's Mum good

Changed her neighborhood.③

Kong Rong good, too,

Modesty he knew.④

【释义 / Paraphrase】

战国时，孟子的母亲善行教子，为使儿子有良好的学习环境，带着他择居三地。三国时代，孔融在 4 岁时即懂得让梨，从小就有谦让的善良品格。

In the Warring States period, Mencius's mother changed her neighborhood three times for better education for her son. During the Three Kingdoms period, Kong Rong had the courtesy to give bigger pears to his elders when he was four.

【注释 / Notes】

①孟子的母亲克勤克俭，含辛茹苦，坚守志节，抚育儿子，为选择良好的环境教育孩子，择居三地，既成就了孟子，更为后世树立起慈母教子的榜样。

②孔融，东汉末年文学家，"建安七子"之一。孔融 4 岁时候，与兄长一起吃梨，他拿了一个最小的梨吃，父亲奇怪地询问他，他回答说："我年纪小，应该吃最小的梨。"他年幼即懂得谦让，受到大家的称赞。《三字经》中有"融四岁，能让梨"之语。

③ In the Warring States period, Mencius's mother moved three times for better environment for her son. Mencius once played truant, and she cut the cloth she was weaving to show her seriousness and the consequences of interrupted learning.

④ In the Han dynasty, Rong (Kong Rong), Confucius's descendant, offered bigger pears to his elder brothers although he was only four. Everyone should learn this kind of respect for affinity.

Three-Word Primer of Goodness
(Chinese–English Bilingual Edition)

wáng xiáng shàn　　qiú lǐ xiān
王祥善，求鲤鲜。①

mù lán shàn　　nǚ bàn nán
木兰善，女扮男。②

Wang Xiang③, why not,

Live carp caught.

Mulan④, then, likewise,

In men's guise.

【释义 / Paraphrase】

三国时的王祥为了让生病的继母吃上鲜鱼，不顾天寒地冻，卧冰求鲤，孝敬继母。南北朝的花木兰女扮男装，替父从军，英勇杀敌，成为巾帼英雄。

In the Three Kingdoms period, regardless of the cold weather, Wang Xiang lay on ice to seek a carp so that his sick stepmother could eat fresh fish. Mulan in the Northern and Southern Dynasties period disguised herself as a man to go to war instead of her father, fought the enemy and became a heroine.

【注释 / Notes】

①王祥，二十四孝中"卧冰求鲤"的主人公，有"孝圣"之称。相传王祥继母朱氏对他并不好，但王祥却更加恭谨。一次，朱氏想吃鲜鱼，当时天寒冰冻，王祥解开衣服，卧在冰上，忽然冰块融化，跃出两条鲤鱼，王祥拿着鲤鱼回去孝敬母亲。朱氏因此深受感动，从此像对亲生儿子那样对他。

②花木兰，中国古代巾帼英雄，忠孝节义，因代父从军击败入侵之敌而流传千古，唐代被追封为"孝烈将军"。

③ Wang Xiang: a figure in "24 Examples of Filial Piety", praised as Sir of Filial Piety. He respected his stepmother who was not good to him. Once in winter, she wanted to eat fresh fish. Wang Xiang took off his clothes and lay on ice. Ice having melted, Wang Xiang caught two carps for his stepmother. Moved by his behavior, she had treated him like her own son since then.

④ Mulan: an ancient Chinese heroine, remembered by going to war in place of her father, disguised as a man. She won the title of General of Filial Piety in the Tang dynasty.

<pre>
liú zǎi shàn   zhōu xiāng juān
刘 宰 善，粥 相 捐。①
lǐ wǔ shàn   chú jí huàn
李 五 善，除 疾 患。②
</pre>

Leader Liu③ good

Offered alms food.

Li Wu④ good

Cured the multitude.

【释义 / Paraphrase】

　　南宋时，刘宰家乡发生饥荒，他慷慨解囊，创办粥局，救济灾民。明代李五为治瘟疫，开仓济糖，将糖倒入井中，任患病之人自取服用，使瘟疫得到了控制。

　　In the Southern Song dynasty, Premier Liu, whose hometown suffered famine, spent money on an alms institution to relieve famine victims. Li Wu, in the Ming dynasty, poured sugar from his sugar hoard to a well so people suffered from the plague could drink the water and be cured.

【注释 / Notes】

　　①刘宰，字平国，南宋江苏金坛人，自号"漫塘病叟"。据《宋史·刘宰传》记载，刘宰为人刚正仁厚，平生多为乡里谋福，是一个"见义必为"之士。创办了中国历史上第一个私人粥局，救济灾民。

　　②李五，原名李英，字俊育，明代泉州晋江凤池人，宣德年间福建著名的慈善家。李五靠生产、贩卖蔗糖致富。明正统九年（1444）浙江宁波瘟疫肆虐，百姓盛传唯有服用凤池糖才可治病，为了让无钱买糖的穷人也及时得到救治，李五当即决定为民舍糖。见需者太多，索性在当地找到一口水井，每天将糖倒入井中，任民众自取服用。不久，瘟疫得到了控制。李五舍糖的那口井被称为"李五恩公井"，直至今日，此井仍存。

　　③ Leader Liu: a good man in the Southern Song dynasty. Upright and kind, he did good to his neighborhood all his life, and set up the first private alms institution for relieving famine victims in the Chinese history.

　　④ Li Wu: Li Ying by original name, a charitarian in the Ming dynasty. To save the poor who had no money for sugar, a good cure, Li Wu poured his own sugar into a well for people who suffered the plague to drink. Before long, the plague was under control, and the well, still preserved today, was called Li Wu's Well.

^{gě fán shàn} ^{gōng shēn jiàn}
葛繁善，躬身践。①

^{xīng zhōu shàn} ^{gōng dé mǎn}
星周善，功德满。②

Ge Fan③ did good

Wherever he could.

Xingzhou④ did good;

Orphans he rescued.

【释义 / Paraphrase】

宋代葛繁秉持善的信念，坚持每天做好事，为人所称道。清代陈文楷为救治弃婴，捐款设育婴堂，朝廷闻听后建牌坊表彰其家族。

Ge Fan in the Song dynasty was praised for his belief in goodness and persisting in performing good deeds every day. Chen Wenkai in the Qing dynasty made donations to establish an orphanage to rescue abandoned babies. The imperial court heard the story and built a memorial gateway to commend his family.

【注释 / Notes】

① 葛繁，号鹤林居士，江苏人。官至镇江太守。坚持每天做好事，力行善事。有人请教他如何"日行一善"，他说："比如这里有条板凳，倒了碍人走路，就弯腰把它扶正放好，即是一善。"

② 陈文楷，字星周，清代慈善家。每逢年关，对孤寡无饭吃的人施以白银，人皆称之为善人。他为了拯救弃婴，斥巨资设育婴堂，救活不少婴儿。后被朝廷以"乐善好施"竖建牌坊旌表其门。

③ Ge Fan: a prefect of Zhenjiang in ancient times. His belief was persisting in performing good deeds every day. He once said, "If there is a bench in the way, put it in the right place, as is a case of goodness."

④ Chen Wenkai: styled Xingzhou, a charitarian in the Qing dynasty. He always gave the poor silver during Spring Festival. In order to rescue abandoned babies, he established an orphanage; therefore the imperial court built a memorial gateway to commend his family.

léi fēng shàn　　ài xīn xiàn
雷锋善，爱心献。①

yù lù shàn　　gōng pú fàn
裕禄善，公仆范。②

Lei Feng③ did good

With love accrued.

Yulu④ did good,

Winning all gratitude.

【释义 / Paraphrase】

中国人民解放军战士雷锋，心怀大爱，无私奉献，助人为乐的事迹广为流传，树起了时代的丰碑。兰考县委书记焦裕禄全心全意为人民服务，忘我工作，以身殉职，成为人民公仆的光辉典范。

As a PLA (Chinese People's Liberation Army) soldier, Lei Feng was famous for his selfless contribution to others, thus a role model of the times. Jiao Yulu, the party secretary of Lankao County, who died on duty, was the best example of serving the people with diligence.

【注释 / Notes】

①雷锋生前是沈阳军区某部战士，曾做过数不清的好人好事，在一次执行任务时因公殉职。毛泽东主席题词："向雷锋同志学习"。"雷锋精神"传颂至今。

②焦裕禄生前任兰考县委书记，他心中时刻装着百姓，唯独没有自己。他"亲民爱民、艰苦奋斗、科学求实、迎难而上、无私奉献"的精神，被后人称为"焦裕禄精神"。

③ Lei Feng: a PLA (Chinese People's Liberation Army) soldier who did countless good deeds and died on duty. His memorial inscription, "Learn from Comrade Lei Feng", was written by Chairman Mao Zedong. Lei Feng's spirit, serving the people, is alive today.

④ Jiao Yulu: a party secretary of Lankao County, who died on duty. "Be good to the people, do good to the country" is known as Jiao Yulu Spirit.

fū qī shàn　　xīng jiā yuán
夫妻善，兴家园。
xiōng dì shàn　　lì kè jiān
兄弟善，力克艰。

A couple good,

No family feud.

All brothers good,

Charge they could.

【释义 / Paraphrase】

夫妻之间只有相亲相爱，相濡以沫，才能使家庭更加兴旺。兄弟之间只有齐心协力，同甘共苦，才能克服一切困难。

Only when a couple love and support each other can they make their family more prosperous. Only by working together and sharing weal and woe can brothers overcome all difficulties.

妯娌善，情谊绵。
子孙善，金不换。

In-laws, if good,

Have better mood.

Posterity, if good,

Live in plenitude.

【释义 / Paraphrase】

　　妯娌之间互敬互让、宽厚包容,才能情意绵绵。子孙善良友爱、奋发有为,是用多少金钱也换不来的。

　　Mutual respect and tolerance among in-laws contribute to a harmonious family relation. Kindness and efforts of posterity is more precious than gold so that they can live in plenitude.

shào nián shàn　　lù píng tǎn
少年善，路平坦。
qīng nián shàn　　jiān zhòng dàn
青年善，肩重担。

Children, if good,

Smooth their road.

Youngsters, if good,

Will nothing elude.

【释义 / Paraphrase】

从小树立正确的人生观,成长之路才会平坦,少走弯路。青年人一身正气,胸怀大志,才能担负起社会的重任。

Setting up a right philosophy of life, children will grow up more smoothly; righteous and aspiring youngsters can take social responsibilities.

zhōng nián shàn　　yì gān dǎn
中年善，益肝胆。

lǎo nián shàn　　shòu yán nián
老年善，寿延年。

Middle-agers, if good,

Rejuvenate they would.

Elders, if good,

Will longevity prelude.

【释义 / Paraphrase】

中年人心中有爱,常行善举,才能有利于成就事业和身心健康。老年人应有善待万物之心,保持平和的心态,才能延年益寿。

Middle-agers, who do good things with love, can have a better career and better physical and mental health; elders, who are good to all, can keep a peaceful mind which can prolong life.

<ruby>睦<rt>mù</rt></ruby><ruby>邻<rt>lín</rt></ruby><ruby>善<rt>shàn</rt></ruby>，<ruby>三<rt>sān</rt></ruby><ruby>尺<rt>chǐ</rt></ruby><ruby>垣<rt>yuán</rt></ruby>。①

<ruby>诫<rt>jiè</rt></ruby><ruby>子<rt>zǐ</rt></ruby><ruby>善<rt>shàn</rt></ruby>，<ruby>大<rt>dà</rt></ruby><ruby>器<rt>qì</rt></ruby><ruby>焉<rt>yān</rt></ruby>。

Be neighbors good,

Not to obtrude.

Be children good,

Rear your magnitude.

【释义 / Paraphrase】

邻里之间应和睦相处，善待他人，克己处事，"六尺巷"的典故已成为彰显和睦谦让美德的见证。三国时期的诸葛亮，以家书告诫儿子静以修身，俭以养德，淡泊明志，努力成为栋梁之材。

Neighbors should be good to each other and deal with problems in a way of self-control, as the allusion of "Six-Foot Lane" has become a sample of harmony and humility. During the Three Kingdoms period, Zhuge Liang taught his son to be good and make contributions to the country.

【注释 / Note】

①六尺巷，位于安徽桐城西后街，全长100多米，宽2米。据载，清康熙时，大学士、礼部尚书张英府第与吴宅为邻。双方为两宅之间的隙地相争，张家人向张英告知此事，张英批诗四句："一纸书来只为墙，让他三尺又何妨。长城万里今犹在，不见当年秦始皇。"张家得诗，让出三尺地基，吴家也效仿退让三尺。两家礼让之举亦被传为美谈。

chuí xùn shàn　　zōng guī yán
垂训善，宗规严。
jiā fēng shàn　　qì xiàng qiān
家风善，气象千。

House teaching good,

Firm family rectitude.

Family tradition good,

Rise all would.

【释义 / Paraphrase】

　　垂训是治理家庭的一项重要内容，宗规是一家一族制定的行为准则，它既有时代的烙印，又有文化的结晶，历史上有很多个家训、族规，影响至今，泽被后世。家庭是社会的基本细胞，人生的第一所学校，好家风可以对几代人带来深远的影响，家庭和善才能幸福美满，人才辈出，气象万千。

　　House teaching is an important part of family management, a code of conduct. With a long tradition, it is an important legacy of culture. Some house teachings in history still have an impact on today's society. Family is the basic cell of the society, the first school of life. A good family tradition can have far-reaching influence on posterity. Only a good family can be happy and foster talents.

<pre>
rén hào shàn   huò qí yuǎn
人好善，祸其远。
quàn xíng shàn   è mò zhān
劝行善，恶莫沾。
</pre>

Be people good,

And evils elude.

Teach what's good,

Nothing bad brood.

【释义 / Paraphrase】

做一个乐善好施的人，灾祸自然离你远去。要经常劝导人们心存善念，多行善事，不要沾染恶习。

When you are happy in doing good, disasters will be away from you. People should be persuaded to be good, do good deeds and give up bad habits.

^{shì shì shàn　　zhì wǔ diǎn}
事事善，志五典①。
^{rì rì shàn　　guì zì rán}
日日善，贵自然。

Everywhere be good,

Never be rude.

Everyday be good,

Be naturally crude.

【释义 / Paraphrase】

善是人性的光芒、品质的展现，用爱心去对待每一件事、每一个人，立志达到"五典"。日行一善，旨在从日常的小事做起，做到知行合一，养成良好的习惯。

Goodness is the light and an expression of human nature. People should be good to everything and everyone, and try to achieve "Five Canons". Doing a good deed every day, people can start from daily things to achieve the unity of knowledge and practice, and develop a good habit.

【注释 / Note】

①五典，古代的五种伦理道德。《尚书·舜典》："慎徽五典，五典克从。"孔传："五典，五常之教。父义、母慈、兄友、弟恭、子孝。"

<pre>
zuò rén shàn   lì biāo gān
做人善，立标杆。
zuò gōng shàn   zhì miǎn jiǎn
做工善，质免检。
</pre>

Be someone good,

Like nectar brewed.

Do craft good,

Exemptions for good.

【释义 / Paraphrase】

　　心地善良、公道正派的人，才能成为人们学习的榜样。用心工作的人，才能打造出高品质的产品，赢得信任和美誉。

　　Kind-hearted and decent people can be good examples. People who work hard can provide high-quality products and win trust and reputation.

gēng zhě shàn　　guǎng liáng tián
耕者善，广良田。
shāng zhě shàn　　wàng cái yuán
商者善，旺财源。

A farmer good,

Reap you would.

A merchant good,

Profit you could.

【释义 / Paraphrase】

　　不辞劳苦、精心耕作的人，才能耕种好广袤的良田，五谷丰登。从商的人只有诚信经营，才能生意兴隆、财源广进。

　　Farmers who are not afraid of hard work can cultivate a vast and fertile land. Only honest businessmen can be prosperous.

dài wù shàn　　lì jié jiǎn
待物善，利节俭。
dài rén shàn　　jié liáng yuán
待人善，结良缘。

To things good,

A frugal livelihood.

To humans good,

A loving brotherhood.

【释义 / Paraphrase】

只有珍惜善待万物,才能有利于养成节俭的良好习惯。与人为善、热心助人的人,才能被大家喜爱,建立起良好的人际关系。

Only by cherishing all can we develop a good habit of thrift. People who are kind and willing to help others can be loved and build good interpersonal relations.

_{chū} _{yǔ} _{shàn}　　_{sān} _{dōng} _{nuǎn}
出语善，三冬暖。

_{yán} _{bù} _{shàn}　　_{liù} _{yuè} _{hán}
言不善，六月寒。

Use words good,

As winter firewood.

Speech not good,

A summer's cold.

【释义 / Paraphrase】

　　说话温和体贴,就是在三九严寒,也会令人感到温暖。恶言恶语,即使是三伏酷暑,也会让人感到寒冷。

　　Good words said, even in the coldest winter, people will feel warm; harsh words said, even in a sweltering summer, one feels cold.

积小善①，汇成潭。

积大善，德如山。

Little good done,

Small streams run!②

Great good done,

Great virtues won.

【释义 / Paraphrase】

　　为善从小事做起，积少成多，就如涓涓细流汇成深潭一样。大的善行善举，表现出的品德像高山一样，令人仰止。

　　Doing good deeds should start from little things—Many a little makes a mickle, just like drops making a deep pool. Great good deeds, like mountains, win people's admiration.

【注释 / Notes】

　　①晋·陈寿《三国志·蜀书·先主传》："勿以恶小而为之，勿以善小而不为。"

　　② Do not commit it because it is a small sin; do not discard it because it is a small pin.

jī zhì shàn　　héng bù biàn
积至善，恒不变。
jī měi shàn　　yú qìng tiān
积美善，余庆添。

Gather what's best,

Succeed without rest.

Beautify what's best,

You'll be blessed.

【释义 / Paraphrase】

至善至美是善的最高境界,追求崇高的善是中华民族几千年来始终如一的信念。崇尚美德,行善积德,必有余庆。

The perfection of goodness and beauty is the highest realm of goodness, as is the consistent pursuit of the Chinese nation for thousands of years. Advocating virtue and doing good deeds, one will be blessed.

wéi yè shàn, rén jiē zàn.
为业善，人皆赞。
wéi mín shàn, tiān dì kuān
为民善，天地宽。

Do work good;

Rise you would.

Do people good;

Win you could.

【释义 / Paraphrase】

对待事业要有工匠精神,精益求精,认真负责,才会得到人们的赞誉。做一个纯朴善良、光明磊落、心存大爱的人,才能达到心底无私天地宽的境界。

For work, only when serious and responsible can one win people's praise; for people, only when loving and aboveboard can one see the great vista of the world.

wéi gōng shàn　　lì qīng lián
为公善，吏清廉。
wéi zhèng shàn　　shèng shì xiàn
为政善，盛世现。

Do public good;

Serve you would.

Do governing good;

Prosper we could.

【释义 / Paraphrase】

为公者心系百姓,甘为公仆,乐于奉献,克己奉公,才能清正廉洁。施政者心系民生,惠民爱民,必将使国家更加繁荣昌盛。

As a civil servant, only when willing to serve the public and having self-control can one do a good job; as an administrator, only when caring for the public and doing them good can one make the country prosperous.

rén xīn shàn　　fēng dù piān
人心善，风度翩。

jǔ guó shàn　　tiān xià huān
举国善，天下欢。

Good your heart,

You are smart.

Good our land,

All happily stand.

【释义 / Paraphrase】

人心向善,从善如流,才会有谦谦君子风度。举国上下政通人和,惠风和畅,百姓才能安居乐业,欢乐祥和。

All people who do good will act in a good manner. When a country is good, the public will live and work happily.

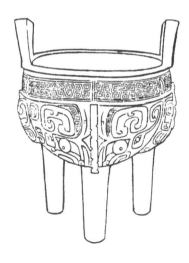

zhōng huá shàn　　jiān rú pán
中华善，坚如磐。

hóng yáng shàn　　zhù mèng yuán
弘扬善，助梦圆。

Our China good,

Stand all would.

What's good extolled,

All strike gold.

【释义 / Paraphrase】

善是中华民族的传统美德,中华民族团结友爱,万众一心,众志成城,坚如磐石。践行社会主义核心价值观,弘扬善文化,将助力于早日实现中国梦。

Goodness is a traditional virtue of the Chinese nation. We Chinese are as strong as rock and unite as one. The practice of socialist core values and the promotion of the culture of goodness will contribute to the achievements of the Chinese Dream.

后 记

善是中国传统文化的主脉络,是中华民族精神的重要标志。古人对善的表述浩如烟海,有光芒四射的千年佳句,有博大精深的专著论述,还有感人至深的人物典范和经典事例。这些厚重的文化积淀是中华文明的重要组成部分,在浩瀚的历史长河中以其独特的魅力影响和激励着人们。

在深受熏陶和启迪的同时,笔者总感觉缺少一种易咏易诵、如诗如歌、朗朗上口、易于传播的载体,为此查阅了大量文献资料、理论文章,编写了《中华善字经》,旨在弘扬善文化,传递正能量,为继承和发扬中国传统文化尽一份绵薄之力。

《中华善字经》自 2017 年 10 月出版发行以来,深受广大读者的关注和好评,至 2019 年 7 月已第 7 次印刷。2018 年 6 月被国家新闻出版署列入《2018 年农家书屋重点出版物推荐目录》,在多地推广普及。连续两年入选第七届、第八届《河北省青少年"阅·知·行"读书活动课外阅读推荐书目》,深得中小学生的喜爱。2019 年 3 月 22 日中央电视台《晚间新闻》对于该书将善文化带进校园进行了专题报道。

　　《中华善字经》汉英对照版的出版发行，得到了上海大学翻译研究出版中心和上海大学出版社的大力支持。在此，感谢上海大学教授、上海大学翻译研究出版中心主任赵彦春亲自为本书进行了巧夺天工的英译；感谢上海大学翻译研究出版中心秘书长许家骏先生策划并统筹了本书的出版；感谢上海大学出版社的陆仕超先生为本书的审稿及联系配音所做的辛勤工作；感谢柯国富先生为本书进行了精美的装帧设计；感谢王悦生先生对稿件进行的审读；感谢华东师范大学外语学院副教授张晴女士、资深外教 Christopher Wolff 先生为本书所做的配音，以及其他所有为本书付梓贡献力量的老师和朋友。

　　惟德动天，无远弗届。在大家的帮助下，善文化走向了更为广阔的交流平台和教育实践并将以其独特的魅力吸引更多读者的关注和研究。

作者

2020 年 4 月

Postscript

Goodness, the artery of traditional Chinese culture, has evolved to be a symbol of the national spirit of China. Our culture is festooned with myriads of expressions of goodness ranging from splendid age-old epigrams or verse lines to extensive and profound monographs and expositions, sparkling with touching paragons like saints and sages and their stories. Such dictums have become a rich legacy, an indispensable thesaurus of Chinese civilization, exerting an indelible impact on the people and inspiring generation upon generation of posterity in the course of history by virtue of their unique charm.

While being deeply influenced and enlightened by the Chinese traditional culture, I think there's a want of a good carrier which is easy to chant and recite, such as poems and songs, and for this purpose I have consulted plenty of literatures including annals and theoretical articles to compose the *Three-Word Primer of Goodness*, aiming at promoting the Goodness Culture and transmitting positive energy, hence making a tiny contribution to the inheritance and glorification of the traditional Chinese culture.

Since its publication in October, 2017, this book has had much attention and praise from the reading public, and has been printed 7 times; in June 2018, it was listed in *The Best Recommended Readers for Framers' Studies, 2018* and was promoted in many places. For two years in succession, it was listed in the Seventh and Eighth *Recommended Ex-curricular Reading·Knowing·Doing Activities for Teenagers in Hebei Province*, well liked by primary and middle school students. On March 22, 2019, the *Evening News* of CCTV reported the Goodness Culture brought to campuses by the book.

The publication of the bilingual edition of the book won the approval and support from Shanghai University Center for Translation and Publishing and Shanghai University Press. Therefore, I take this opportunity to express my thanks.

I feel indebted to Professor Zhao Yanchun, Director of Shanghai University Center for Translation and Publishing for his hermetic translation of the book; I would like to express my sincere gratitude to Mr. Xu Jiajun, Secretary-general of Shanghai University Center for Translation and Publishing, for his planning and deep involvement; my thanks also go to Mr. Lu Shichao at Shanghai University Press for his valuable contribution to reviewing this book and contacting dubbers; I also thank Mr. Ke Guofu for his quality binding designing for this book; I also express my thanks to Mr. Wang Yuesheng for his careful proofreading; and I have a sincere sense of gratitude to Associate Professor Zhang Qing and Mr. Christopher Wolff at Foreign Language School of East China Normal University for their dubbing as well as all the other teachers and friends for their significant contribution to this book.

It is virtue that touches the sky, though it looms yonder, far and high. With the joint efforts of everyone, the Goodness culture has stepped onto the stage for academic exchanges and educational development, and will draw more readers' attention to its research with its unique charm.

The Author
April, 2020

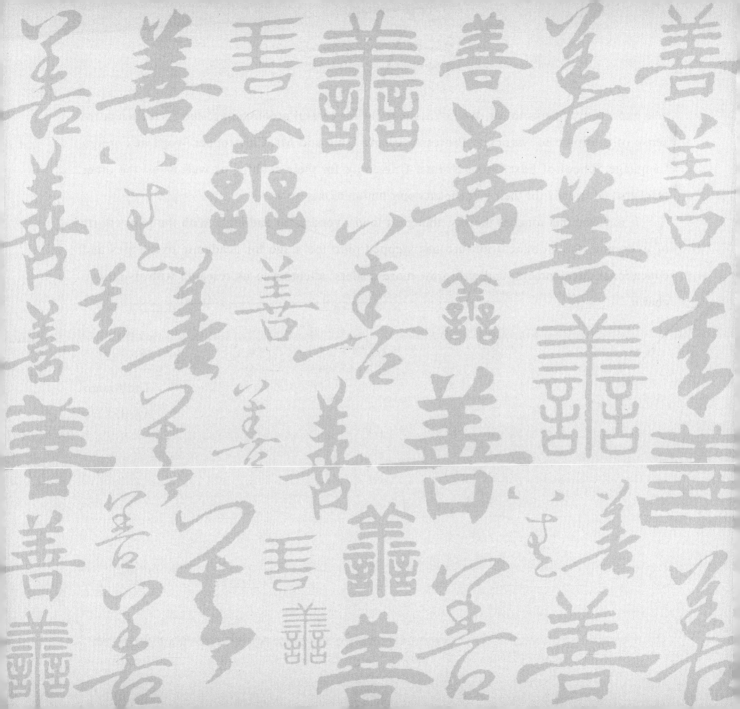